Muffins & Quick Breads

GENERAL EDITOR
Chuck Williams

RECIPES
John Phillip Carroll

PHOTOGRAPHY
Allan Rosenberg

TIME
LIFE
BOOKS

TIME-LIFE BOOKS
Time-Life Books is a division of Time Life Inc.
Time-Life is a trademark of Time Warner Inc. U.S.A.

A Note on Weights and Measures:
All recipes include customary U.S. and metric measurements. Metric conversions are based on a standard developed for these books and have been rounded off. Actual weights may vary.

Time-Life Custom Publishing
Vice President and Publisher: Terry Newell
Managing Editor: Donia Ann Steele
Director of New Product Development:
    Quentin McAndrew
Director of Sales: Neil Levin
Director of Financial Operations: J. Brian Birky

WILLIAMS-SONOMA
Founder/Vice-Chairman: Chuck Williams
Book Buyer: Victoria Kalish

WELDON OWEN INC.
President: John Owen
Publisher: Wendely Harvey
Managing Editor: Laurie Wertz
Consulting Editor: Norman Kolpas
Copy Editor: Sharon Silva
Editorial Assistant: Janique Poncelet
Design: John Bull, The Book Design Company
Production: Stephanie Sherman, James Obata,
    Mick Bagnato
Production Coordinator: Tarji Mickelson
Co-Editions Director: Derek Barton
Food Photographer: Allan Rosenberg
Additional Food Photography: Allen V. Lott
Primary Food & Prop Stylist: Sandra Griswold
Food Stylist: Heidi Gintner
Assistant Food Stylist: Danielle Di Salvo
Prop Assistant: Karen Nicks
Glossary Illustrations: Alice Harth

The Williams-Sonoma Kitchen Library
conceived and produced by Weldon Owen Inc.
814 Montgomery St., San Francisco, CA 94133

In collaboration with Williams-Sonoma
3250 Van Ness Ave., San Francisco, CA 94109

Printed in China

A Weldon Owen Production

Copyright © 1993 Weldon Owen Inc.
Reprinted in 1993; 1993; 1993; 1993; 1993; 1994; 1994;
    1995; 1995; 1995; 1996; 1997; 1997

Library of Congress
Cataloging-in-Publication Data:

Carroll, John Phillip.
    Muffins & quick breads / general editor,
    Chuck Williams ; recipes, John Phillip Carroll ;
    photography, Allan Rosenberg.
                p.   cm. — (Williams-Sonoma kitchen library)
    Includes index.
    ISBN 0-7835-0233-8 (trade) ;
    ISBN 0-7835-0234-6
    1. Muffins.   2. Bread.   I. Williams, Chuck.   II. Title.
III. Title: Muffins and quick breads.
IV. Series.
TX770.M83C37   1993
641.8'15—dc20   92-27837
                                                      CIP

Contents

SWEET MUFFINS 17

SWEET QUICK BREADS 53

SAVORY MUFFINS 69

SAVORY QUICK BREADS 85

INTRODUCTION

Imagine, for a moment, the pleasure of serving your family and friends fresh-baked breads, hot from your oven.

Yet many cooks shy away from baking, considering it a time-consuming process that yields unpredictable results. How wrong they are, especially when you consider how easy it is to make muffins and quick breads. Leavened by baking powder, muffin and quick bread batters are mixed in minutes and bake in less than a half hour for muffins, and no more than an hour for quick breads. They are, quite literally, the easiest breads to make.

This volume shows you just how easy muffin baking can be. It begins with the basics, from kitchen equipment—most of which you probably already have—and simple steps for mixing and baking batters, to a few classic spreads and toppings for serving along with your just-baked breads. The rest of the book is dedicated to 44 recipes that demonstrate the incredible variety this simplest form of baking offers.

Variety is the key word here. Most cooks think of muffins and quick breads merely as foods to serve at breakfast, brunch or teatime. Yet, you'll find many recipes here for savory breads well suited to lunch or dinner: muffins to accompany soups or stews, loaves you can toast and use for sandwiches. That versatility also extends to the fact that virtually any muffin batter in this book can be baked as a quick bread, and vice versa. All you have to do is adjust the baking time.

Once you've tried a recipe or two—and I hope you will right away—I'm sure you'll be impressed with just how easy home baking can be.

Chuck Williams

EQUIPMENT

Simple tools for the quick and easy tasks of mixing, shaping and baking muffins and quick breads

More likely than not, every home cook already has all the equipment necessary to make a batch of muffins or a loaf of quick bread.

Measuring tools make it easy to achieve the proper proportions. And virtually any mixing bowls and stirrers will do the job of combining the ingredients.

Muffin tins or loaf pans such as those shown here allow you to bake breads in a variety of sizes. If you like, seek out unusual muffin shapes—hearts, ears of corn, scallops—to add a more personal touch to your baking.

1. Mixing Bowls
Choose high-sided, deep bowls for easier mixing. Large bowl holds dry ingredients. Smaller bowl, for liquid ingredients, has a lip for pouring.

2. Loaf Pans
For baking quick breads in large, medium and miniature sizes. The recipes in this book use either a large loaf pan, which measures 9 x 5 x 3 inches (23 x 13 x 7.5 cm) and holds 8 cups (64 fl oz/2 l), or a medium pan, which measures 8½ x 4½ x 2½ inches (21 x 11 x 6 cm) and holds 6 cups (48 fl oz/1.5 l). You can also use a miniature pan, which generally measures 6 x 3 x 2 inches (15 x 7.5 x 5 cm) and holds about 2 cups (16 fl oz/ 500 ml). Metal pans—here, tinned steel (large pan), dark stick-resistant aluminum (medium) and standard aluminum (mini)—all conduct heat well; the dark pan absorbs heat faster, so the baking temperature may have to be decreased by 25°F (15°C).

3. Round Loaf Pan
Other baking pans, such as the circular springform pan shown here, a square cake pan or a ring-shaped tube pan, may be used to make different loaf shapes.

4. Rubber Spatula
For scraping batters out of mixing bowls and for smoothing surfaces of batters in loaf pans. Choose sturdy, pliable rubber or silicone heads.

5. Flat Whisk
Flat, open arrangement of wires mixes batters quickly and thoroughly.

6. Wooden Spoon

Traditional tool of choice for mixing batters. Choose a good-quality spoon with a sturdy handle.

7. Metal Spatula

Long, straight blade levels the surface of dry ingredients with the rims of measuring cups for accuracy.

8. Chef's Knife

For general slicing, cutting and chopping of ingredients, and for slicing baked loaves. Select a good-quality stain-resistant steel blade with a firmly anchored, comfortable handle.

9. Zest Grater

Small, sturdy, stainless-steel grating surface for finely grated citrus zest.

10. Zester

Small, sharp holes at end of stainless-steel blade cut citrus zest into fine shreds. Choose a model with a sturdy, well-attached handle.

11. Wooden Toothpicks

Choose wooden toothpicks for inserting into muffins to test them for doneness. For quick bread recipes, use a long, thin wooden skewer.

12. Muffin Tins

Tins for baking miniature (about 1½ tablespoons), standard (about 3½ fl oz/110 ml) and oversized (about ¾ cup/ 6 fl oz/180 ml) muffins. Small muffins may take a few minutes less to bake, oversized a few minutes more. Whenever possible, choose stick-resistant tins. If the tins have dark surfaces, which absorb heat more easily, this may require lowering the temperature by 25°F (15°C) or baking for a shorter time.

13. Wire Cooling Rack

Allows air to circulate under baked muffins and loaves for quick, even cooling. Choose racks with closely spaced wires.

14. Pot Holder and Oven Mitt

For removing muffin and loaf pans from the oven. Made of heavy, quilted cotton for good protection from heat, with one side of pot holder treated for fire resistance.

15. Liquid Measuring Cup

For accurate measuring of liquid ingredients. Choose heavy-duty heat-resistant glass, marked on one side in cups and ounces, on the other in milliliters. Lip and handle allow for easy pouring.

16. Measuring Spoons

In graduated sizes, for measuring small quantities of ingredients such as baking powder and salt. Select good-quality, calibrated metal spoons with deep bowls.

17. Dry Measuring Cups

In graduated sizes, for accurate measuring of dry ingredients. Straight rims allow ingredients to be leveled for accuracy. Choose stainless steel for accuracy and sturdiness.

18. Wire Whisk

For beating eggs or blending liquids before incorporating them into batters. Choose stainless steel.

MUFFIN-BAKING BASICS

Six simple steps ensure golden, tender, moist and fragrant muffins every time you bake them

The ease of muffin making is vividly illustrated by the six photographs shown at right for classic blueberry muffins (see recipe on page 36): preparing the muffin tin, mixing dry and liquid ingredients, stirring the batter, filling the muffin tin, and baking and testing for doneness.

Of course, some added insights will speed you along the path to producing perfect muffins. Preparing the tin, for example, is a step that, although simple, sometimes gets scant attention. Coating the cups thoroughly with butter keeps the muffins from sticking; since it also promotes their browning, the step is recommended even for stick-resistant cookware. If you're watching your cholesterol or fats, substitute margarine or vegetable shortening; or use a nonstick cooking spray, making sure each muffin cup is evenly coated. And if you would like the homey touch of paper muffin cups, by all means line the tins with them, omitting the greasing step.

When blending the batter, take special care not to overmix it—an error that overdevelops the flour's gluten and promotes toughness. A light hand, sometimes resulting in a slightly lumpy batter, yields the most tender muffins.

Since many home ovens cook hotter or cooler than the temperatures to which they are set, it is also wise to calibrate your oven. Place a good-quality oven thermometer on the center rack and use the temperature it registers as your guide to adjusting the heat.

The recipes in this book call for a standard muffin tin (6-tablespoon/3½-fl oz/110-ml cup capacity), usually yielding 12 muffins. If you bake the batter in

1. Buttering the tins.
First, preheat the oven to the temperature called for in the recipe. To prevent muffins from sticking, prepare the tin by lightly but thoroughly coating the cups with softened butter, using a paper towel, if you like, to keep your fingers clean.

2. Mixing the dry ingredients.
Measure all the dry ingredients—flour, sugar, baking powder or soda, salt and other seasonings—and put them in a large mixing bowl. With a flat whisk, wooden spoon or other implement, stir well to combine the ingredients thoroughly.

oversized or miniature muffin tins, the yield will vary. So will baking times, with oversized muffins taking a few minutes longer to bake completely, and miniatures a few minutes less; be sure to test for doneness.

Finally, if you have only one muffin tin, bake the batter in batches; the batter will keep at room temperature until the first batch of muffins is done.

3. Mixing the liquid ingredients.
In another mixing bowl, whisk together the liquid ingredients—such as milk or cream, eggs, melted butter and oil—until thoroughly combined.

4. Stirring the batter.
Combine the liquid and dry ingredients and stir just until the batter is blended. A few lumps are okay; do not overmix or the muffins may be tough.

5. Filling the muffin cups.
Just before filling the cups, add any solid ingredients—in this case, blueberries—and stir briefly until incorporated. Spoon the batter into the prepared muffin cups, filling them to the depth called for in the recipe—usually two-thirds to three-quarters full. Place the muffin tin on the middle rack of the preheated oven.

6. Testing for doneness.
Check the muffins when the minimum baking time called for in the recipe has elapsed. If they are well risen and golden, test for doneness by inserting a wooden toothpick into the center of one muffin. If it comes out clean, the muffins are done; if some batter clings to the toothpick, bake a few more minutes before testing again. Cool in the tin for a few minutes, then remove.

Quick Bread Basics

Any muffin batter can be baked in a loaf pan or other deep baking pan to make a quick bread— just as any quick bread batter can be baked in a muffin tin.

But, because of the longer baking time a quick bread loaf requires, its pan demands a different preparation to ensure that the bread does not stick or scorch. The pan is thoroughly greased like the individual cups of a muffin tin, using either butter or vegetable shortening, and then lightly coated with flour.

Baking and testing for doneness proceeds in the same way as shown for muffins on the previous page. Once a loaf of quick bread is done, however, it is usually unmolded from its pan to cool on a wire rack so that its crust remains firm and crisp.

1. Greasing and flouring.
First, preheat the oven to the temperature called for in the recipe. To prevent a quick bread from sticking, prepare the loaf pan by lightly but thoroughly coating the interior with softened butter or shortening, using a paper towel, if you like, to keep your fingers clean. Then add a small scoop of all-purpose (plain) flour and tilt and shake the pan to leave a light, even coating of flour on the butter. Tip the pan to shake out the excess flour.

2. Spreading the batter.
Prepare the batter and transfer to the pan. Lightly tap the pan on a work surface to eliminate any air pockets. Using a rubber spatula, smooth the batter so the loaf rises and browns evenly during baking. Place the pan in the preheated oven.

3. Unmolding and cooling.
When the loaf is well risen and golden, insert a thin wooden skewer into its center to test for doneness. When the skewer comes out clean, remove the pan from the oven. Cool in the pan for 10 minutes, then unmold the loaf; if it sticks, run a narrow metal spatula around the sides. Transfer the loaf right side up to a wire rack to cool.

Fine Grating for Fresh Flavors

Citrus zests and fresh ginger are among the most vivid flavorings for muffins and quick breads. A zester produces fine shreds; a hand-held grater, smaller particles. Any sturdy grater will handle fresh ginger, although a ginger grater tackles the fibrous flesh best.

Finely shredding zest.
To produce fine shreds of citrus zest, hold the fruit securely in one hand and, with the other, draw the cutting holes of a special citrus zester across the surface of the fruit.

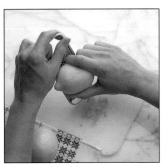

Finely grating zest.
For finely grated citrus zest, use one hand to steady a fine-holed, sturdy grater on a nonslip work surface. With the other hand, lightly but firmly grate the citrus fruit, turning it frequently to avoid grating any bitter white pith.

Grating fresh ginger.
Use a special ginger grater or the medium-sized grating surface of a hand-held grater. Using a small, sharp knife, trim one end of the ginger and peel off some of the papery brown skin before grating.

ADDING SOMETHING EXTRA

Muffins and quick breads are easily enhanced with a few simple flourishes.

A sweet crumble topping (see recipe on page 24) adds an attractive, crunchy crust. You could also add such toppings as sugar crystals or cinnamon sugar (see pages 26 and 61).

Still other treats may be hidden *inside* muffins, such as the jam in the strawberry-orange muffins on page 30. Chopped chocolate, cream cheese or chunks of ripe summer fruit are other good choices.

Hiding a dab of jam.
Fill prepared muffin cups less than half full with batter. Place a dab of jam in the center of each cup. Then add more batter to fill cups two-thirds full, concealing jam.

Sugar syrup saturates a quick bread with flavor and texture. Besides the lemon syrup on page 58, you could use syrups flavored with other juices or sweet spices.

Adding a crumble topping.
To make the crumble topping, use your fingertips to combine flour, sugar, salt, sweet spices and shortening, producing a mixture resembling bread crumbs. After filling muffin cups with batter, sprinkle a scant tablespoon of topping over each cup.

Drizzling with syrup.
Prepare a simple sugar syrup—in this case, flavored with fresh lemon juice. Poke holes all over the bread's surface and drizzle the syrup over it. Let cool for 15 minutes before unmolding.

Basic Glaze

A thin coating of glaze adds a flair to muffins and quick breads. Orange is sweet and bright; lemon glaze contributes a pleasant tartness. Either one would be good on any of the sweet, fruity breads and muffins in this book.

FOR THE ORANGE GLAZE:
1 cup (4 oz/125 g) confectioners' (icing) sugar, sifted
2 tablespoons fresh orange juice, or more if needed
2 teaspoons orange zest
pinch of salt

FOR THE LEMON GLAZE:
1 cup (4 oz/125 g) confectioners' (icing) sugar, sifted
2 tablespoons fresh lemon juice, or more if needed
2 teaspoons lemon zest
pinch of salt

Combine all the ingredients for either glaze in a small bowl and whisk briskly until smooth and well blended. If the glaze is too stiff, beat in a few drops more juice. Brush or spoon over breads and muffins while they are still warm.

Makes about ¼ cup (2 fl oz/60 ml), enough for 12 muffins or 1 loaf of bread

Orange Glaze

Lemon Glaze

Uncooked Strawberry Jam

No cooking, no canning and very little mess. Jam doesn't get any easier than this—just mashed fruit and sugar perked up with lemon juice. The color is beautiful and the flavor fresh and sweet, making it a good foil for some of the rich, fine-textured breads, such as oatmeal-raisin (recipe on page 57), holiday fruit (page 66) or sour cream–raisin (page 61). Although the yield is quite small, the jam takes only minutes to make, and you can alter the recipe with other berries, or by adding chopped nuts or grated lemon or orange zest.

2 baskets strawberries (1½ lb/750 g total weight), stemmed
⅓–½ cup (3–4 oz/90–125 g) sugar
1–2 tablespoons fresh lemon juice

*P*lace the berries in a bowl and mash them to a pulp. Add the sugar and lemon juice to taste (fruit that is very ripe and flavorful will need the smaller amounts of sugar and lemon juice). Let sit for 1 hour, stirring occasionally. Cover and store in the refrigerator for up to 5 days.

*Makes about 2 cups
(22 oz/680 g)*

Pear-Ginger Jam

This jam has a spicy, fresh flavor. It is marvelous on both sweet and savory breads and muffins, especially those made with whole grains, nuts and seeds. Try it on a slice of lightly toasted whole-wheat walnut bread (recipe on page 88). To store, place the jam in a jar, press a piece of plastic wrap directly onto the surface of the jam, cover with a tight cap and refrigerate for up to 3 days. The surface will gradually darken slightly, so stir before serving.

3 ripe pears (about 1½ lb/750 g total weight), such as Bartletts, peeled, cored and cut into chunks
½ cup (4 oz/125 g) sugar
3 tablespoons fresh lemon juice
1 tablespoon finely grated fresh ginger

*I*n a food processor fitted with the metal blade, purée the pears until smooth. Add all the remaining ingredients and process briefly to mix.

Makes about 1½ cups (1 lb/500 g)

Pear-Ginger Jam

Uncooked Strawberry Jam

Strawberry Jam Butter

In only a few seconds, you have a delicious fruit butter with a good berry flavor, just right for any citrus-flavored muffin or bread. The powdered milk, incidentally, absorbs the moisture in the jam and prevents the mixture from forming rivulets of separation. A food processor is the best tool for making the smoothest butter.

½ cup (4 oz/125 g) unsalted butter, at room
    temperature
2 tablespoons nonfat dry milk (milk powder)
⅓ cup (3 oz/90 g) strawberry jam
½ cup (2 oz/60 g) confectioners' (icing) sugar
pinch of salt

*I*n a food processor fitted with the metal blade, process the butter until smooth and light, scraping down the work bowl once or twice. Add 1 tablespoon of the dry milk, the jam and sugar and process until blended. Add the remaining 1 tablespoon dry milk and the salt and process until smooth, scraping down the work bowl once or twice.

Store tightly covered in the refrigerator for up to 1 week; bring to room temperature before serving.

Makes about 1 cup (8 oz/250 g)

Strawberry Jam Butter

Savory Butters

Here are two compound butters, both of which are good spread on savory muffins and breads. The tomato-basil blend is bright, fragrant and summery—a nice companion to both cottage cheese muffins (recipe on page 82) and sun-dried tomato–herb muffins (page 79). The strongly flavored, piquant caper-mustard butter is especially good on whole-grain breads and muffins; try it with buckwheat kasha bread (page 99).

FOR TOMATO-BASIL BUTTER:
½ cup (4 oz/125 g) unsalted butter, at room
    temperature
3 tablespoons tomato paste
2 tablespoons chopped fresh basil or 2 teaspoons
    dried basil
½ teaspoon salt

FOR CAPER-MUSTARD BUTTER:
½ cup (4 oz/125 g) unsalted butter, at room
    temperature
2 tablespoons chopped, well-drained capers
2 tablespoons Dijon mustard
¼ teaspoon salt
¼ teaspoon freshly ground pepper

Combine all the ingredients for either butter in a food processor fitted with the metal blade. Process until smooth and blended, scraping down the sides of the work bowl two or three times. Scrape into a small bowl. Alternatively, using a wooden spoon beat together all the ingredients in a small bowl until completely mixed. Cover and refrigerate for up to 1 week; bring to room temperature before serving.

Makes about ¾ cup (6 oz/185 g)

Tomato-Basil Butter

Caper-Mustard Butter

Orange-Yogurt Muffins

3 large oranges
½ cup (4 oz/125 g) sugar
2 tablespoons water
5 tablespoons (2½ oz/80 g) unsalted butter
2 cups (10 oz/315 g) all-purpose (plain) flour
1¼ teaspoons baking powder
1 teaspoon baking soda (bicarbonate of soda)
½ teaspoon salt
2 eggs
¾ cup (6 oz/185 g) plain yogurt
¾ cup (6 fl oz/180 ml) milk

A generous measure of grated orange zest gives these muffins an extraordinary taste, and cooking the zest briefly with a small amount of sugar is one of the best ways to extract its flavor. While the muffins are baking, squeeze the juice from one of the oranges to make the orange glaze on page 12.

Preheat an oven to 375°F (190°C). Butter standard muffin tins.

Finely grate the zest from the oranges, removing only the bright orange portion of the peel. You should have about ¼ cup (1 oz/30 g) of zest. Combine the zest, ¼ cup (2 oz/60 g) of the sugar and the water in a small saucepan. Stir over medium heat for about 2 minutes, until the sugar dissolves. Add the butter and stir until melted, about 1 minute more. Set aside.

In a medium bowl stir and toss together the flour, baking powder, baking soda, salt and the remaining ¼ cup (2 oz/65 g) sugar. Set aside. In a larger bowl whisk together the eggs, yogurt, milk and reserved orange mixture until smooth. Add the combined dry ingredients and stir just until blended.

Spoon into the prepared muffin tins, filling each cup about three-quarters full. Bake until a toothpick inserted in the center of a muffin comes out clean, 15–20 minutes. Cool in the tins for 3 minutes, then remove.

Makes about 18 standard muffins

Banana-Bran Muffins

1 cup (5 oz/155 g) all-purpose (plain) flour

1 cup (2½ oz/80 g) wheat bran

1 teaspoon baking soda (bicarbonate of soda)

½ teaspoon salt

½ cup (2 oz/60 g) chopped walnuts or pecans

1 cup (8 oz/250 g) mashed ripe banana (2 large bananas)

½ cup (4 oz/125 g) unsalted butter, at room temperature

½ cup (3½ oz/105 g) firmly packed brown sugar

1 egg

Use only bananas that are fully ripe (the skins should be speckled with brown). After peeling, mash them vigorously with a potato masher to a smooth pulp. These muffins are moist and sweet, with an honest banana flavor.

Preheat an oven to 375°F (190°C). Butter standard muffin tins.

In a medium bowl stir and toss together the flour, bran, baking soda, salt and nuts. Set aside. In another medium bowl beat together the banana and butter until mixed—don't worry if the mixture looks lumpy and curdled—then add the brown sugar and egg and beat until completely mixed. Add the combined dry ingredients and stir just until blended.

Spoon into the prepared muffin tins, filling each cup about three-quarters full. Bake until a toothpick inserted in the center of a muffin comes out clean, 15–20 minutes. Cool in the tins for 5 minutes, then remove.

Makes about 12 standard muffins

Marion Cunningham's Fresh Ginger Muffins

1 piece fresh ginger, 4–5 oz
(125–155 g), unpeeled

¾ cup (6 oz/185 g) plus 3 tablespoons
sugar

2 tablespoons finely grated lemon zest

2 cups (10 oz/315 g) all-purpose
(plain) flour

½ teaspoon salt

¾ teaspoon baking soda (bicarbonate
of soda)

½ cup (4 oz/125 g) unsalted butter,
at room temperature

2 eggs

1 cup (8 fl oz/250 ml) buttermilk

One of the best muffins ever, from the author of The Breakfast Book *and* The Supper Book *and the person we must thank for revising* The Fannie Farmer Cookbook *for our generation. These are good with the pear-ginger jam on page 13.*

Preheat an oven to 375°F (190°C). Butter standard muffin tins. Cut the unpeeled ginger into large chunks. In a food processor fitted with the metal blade, process until it is finely minced (or chop finely by hand). You should have about ¼ cup (2 oz/60 g). In a small saucepan combine the ginger and ¼ cup (2 oz/60 g) of the sugar and cook over medium heat, stirring, until the sugar melts and the mixture is hot; this takes only a couple minutes. Set aside to cool until tepid.

Stir the lemon zest and the 3 tablespoons sugar together in a small bowl. Let stand for a few minutes, then add to the ginger mixture. Stir and set aside.

In a medium bowl stir and toss together the flour, salt and baking soda. Set aside. In a large bowl, beat the butter until smooth. Add the remaining ½ cup (4 oz/ 125 g) sugar and beat until blended. Add the eggs and beat well. Add the buttermilk and mix until blended. Then add the combined dry ingredients and stir just until blended. Stir in the ginger-lemon mixture.

Spoon into the tins, filling about three-quarters full. Bake until a toothpick comes out clean, 15–20 minutes. Cool in the tins for 1 minute, then remove.

Makes about 16 standard muffins

Lemon Slice Muffins

3 lemons
1 tablespoon water
about ½ cup (4 oz/125 g) sugar
6 tablespoons (3 oz/90 g) unsalted
 butter
2 cups (10 oz/315 g) all-purpose
 (plain) flour
2 teaspoons baking powder
½ teaspoon baking soda (bicarbonate
 of soda)
½ teaspoon salt
2 eggs
1 cup (8 fl oz/250 ml) milk

Serve these muffins warm, with the bottoms upturned so the glazed lemon slice is visible.

❋

Preheat an oven to 400°F (200°C). Butter standard muffin tins.

Finely grate the zest from the lemons, removing only the bright yellow portion of the peel. Set the lemons aside. Combine the zest, the water and ¼ cup (2 oz/60 g) of the sugar in a small saucepan. Stir over medium heat for about 2 minutes, just until the sugar dissolves. Add the butter and stir until melted, about 1 minute longer. Set aside.

With a sharp knife remove and discard all the remaining peel from the lemons. Cut the lemons crosswise into slices about ¼ inch (6 mm) thick; discard any seeds. You will need about 12 nicely shaped slices. Put about 1 teaspoon of the remaining sugar in the bottom of each prepared muffin cup and place a lemon slice on top.

In a medium bowl stir and toss together the flour, baking powder, baking soda and salt. Set aside. In a larger bowl whisk together the eggs, milk and the reserved lemon mixture until smooth. Add the combined dry ingredients and stir just until blended.

Spoon into the tins, filling about three-quarters full. Bake until a toothpick comes out clean, 15–20 minutes. Immediately invert the tins onto a wire rack. Cool in the tins for 5 minutes, then lift away the tins; the muffins should fall out. If they resist, nudge them with a knife.

Makes about 12 standard muffins

Cinnamon Crunch Muffins

3 cups (15 oz/470 g) all-purpose (plain) flour

1½ cups (10½ oz/330 g) firmly packed brown sugar

½ teaspoon salt

2 teaspoons ground cinnamon

1 teaspoon ground ginger

⅔ cup (5 oz/155 g) vegetable shortening

½ cup (2 oz/60 g) chopped pecans or walnuts

2 teaspoons baking powder

½ teaspoon baking soda (bicarbonate of soda)

2 eggs, beaten

1 cup (8 fl oz/250 ml) buttermilk

These will remind you of a spicy coffeecake with streusel topping. They are good warm or cold, and the recipe makes plenty, so you can bake them for Sunday breakfast and enjoy them during the week, too. Serve them with strawberry jam butter (recipe on page 14).

Preheat an oven to 375°F (190°C). Butter standard muffin tins.

In a large bowl stir and toss together the flour, sugar, salt, 1 teaspoon of the cinnamon and the ginger. Add the shortening and mix the ingredients together—your fingertips are good tools for this job—until thoroughly combined and crumbly. Remove ⅔ cup (3 oz/90 g) of the mixture to a small bowl and mix the nuts and the remaining teaspoon of cinnamon into it. Set aside to use for the topping.

To the remaining flour mixture, add the baking powder and baking soda and stir and toss to combine. Add the eggs and buttermilk and stir just until blended.

Spoon into the prepared muffin tins, filling each cup about two-thirds full. Sprinkle each muffin with about 1 tablespoon of the reserved topping. Bake until a toothpick inserted in the center of a muffin comes out clean, 15–20 minutes. Cool in the tins for 3 minutes, then remove.

Makes about 18 standard muffins

Currant Muffins

FOR THE TOPPING:
¼ cup (2 oz/60 g) sugar
1 teaspoon ground cinnamon

FOR THE BATTER:
1½ cups (7½ oz/235 g) all-purpose
  (plain) flour
¼ cup (2 oz/60 g) sugar
1 teaspoon baking soda (bicarbonate
  of soda)
½ teaspoon baking powder
½ teaspoon salt
¾ cup (6 fl oz/180 ml) buttermilk
6 tablespoons (3 oz/90 g) unsalted
  butter, melted
1 egg
¼ cup (2½ oz/75 g) orange marmalade
½ cup (3 oz/90 g) dried currants

Currants are wonderful, full of flavor and sweetness. Even a small amount of them in a batter can seem like an abundance. These muffins have a cinnamon-sugar topping, and will remind you of a coffee cake.

Preheat an oven to 375°F (190°C). Butter standard muffin tins.

To make the topping, combine the sugar and cinnamon in a small cup and set aside.

To make the batter, in a medium bowl stir and toss together the flour, sugar, baking soda, baking powder and salt. Set aside. In another medium bowl whisk together the buttermilk, melted butter, egg, marmalade and currants until smooth. Add to the combined dry ingredients and stir just until blended.

Spoon into the prepared muffin tins, filling each cup about three-quarters full. Sprinkle each muffin with about 1 teaspoon of the topping. Bake until a toothpick inserted in the center of a muffin comes out clean, about 15 minutes. Cool in the tins for a moment, then remove.

Makes about 12 standard muffins

Bran Muffins

2½ cups (6½ oz/200 g) wheat bran
1½ cups (7½ oz/235 g) whole-wheat
   (wholemeal) flour
¼ cup (2 oz/60 g) firmly packed
   brown sugar
2½ teaspoons baking soda
   (bicarbonate of soda)
1 teaspoon salt
4 eggs
1 cup (8 fl oz/250 ml) buttermilk
⅓ cup (3 fl oz/80 ml) vegetable oil
¼ cup (3 oz/90 g) molasses
¼ cup (3 oz/90 g) honey
1 cup (6 oz/185 g) raisins

Moist, flavorful, dark and slightly sweet—and they give you a good measure of fiber, too. The recipe makes a lot; uneaten muffins may be stored in a tightly sealed plastic bag for several days.

❋

*P*reheat an oven to 400°F (200°C). Butter standard muffin tins.

In a large bowl stir and toss together the bran, flour, brown sugar, baking soda and salt. Set aside. In another bowl whisk together the eggs, buttermilk, oil, molasses and honey until smooth. Stir in the raisins. Add to the combined dry ingredients and stir just until blended.

Spoon into the prepared muffin tins, filling each cup about two-thirds full. Bake until a toothpick inserted in the center of a muffin comes out clean, about 15 minutes. Cool in the tins for 3 minutes, then remove.

Makes about 24 standard muffins

Strawberry-Orange Muffins

2¼ cups (11½ oz/360 g) all-purpose (plain) flour

2 teaspoons baking powder

1 teaspoon baking soda (bicarbonate of soda)

½ teaspoon salt

¾ cup (6 oz/185 g) sugar

½ cup (4 fl oz/125 ml) milk

½ cup (4 fl oz/125 ml) sour cream

⅓ cup (3 fl oz/80 ml) vegetable oil

1 egg

1 tablespoon finely grated orange zest

1 cup (4 oz/125 g) thinly sliced fresh strawberries

about ⅓ cup (4 oz/125 g) strawberry jam

Slice the berries very thinly—about ⅛ inch (3 mm) if you can—then pat the slices dry between paper towels, to keep their juices from coloring the batter. These muffins also have a surprise: a dab of strawberry jam hidden in the center.

Preheat an oven to 400°F (200°C). Butter standard muffin tins.

In a large bowl stir and toss together the flour, baking powder, baking soda and salt. Set aside. In a medium bowl whisk together the sugar, milk, sour cream, oil, egg and orange zest until mixed, stir in the strawberries. Add to the combined dry ingredients and stir just until blended.

Place a spoonful of batter in each prepared muffin cup. Top each with a scant teaspoon of strawberry jam. Spoon the remaining batter over the jam, filling each cup about two-thirds full. Bake until a toothpick inserted in the center of a muffin comes out clean, 15–18 minutes. Cool in the tins for 5 minutes, then remove.

Makes about 16 standard muffins

Oat Bran Muffins

2 cups (5 oz/160 g) oat bran
1 cup (5 oz/155 g) all-purpose (plain)
 flour
½ cup (3½ oz/105 g) firmly packed
 brown sugar
4 teaspoons baking powder
1 teaspoon ground cinnamon
½ teaspoon salt
1¼ cups (10 fl oz/310 ml) milk
2 eggs
⅓ cup (3 fl oz/80 ml) vegetable oil
½ cup (3 oz/90 g) raisins

Oat bran muffins are lighter and more cakelike than those made with wheat bran. This recipe takes well to all kinds of additions, especially chopped dried fruit such as apricots, pears or prunes; add up to 1 cup (6 oz/185 g) of any of these suggestions.

Preheat an oven to 425°F (220°C). Butter standard muffin tins.

In a large bowl stir and toss together the oat bran, flour, sugar, baking powder, cinnamon and salt. Set aside. In a small bowl whisk together the milk, eggs and oil until smooth. Stir in the raisins. Add to the combined dry ingredients and stir just until blended.

Spoon into the prepared muffin tins, filling each cup about two-thirds full. Bake until a toothpick inserted in the center of a muffin comes out clean, 15–18 minutes. Cool in the tins for 3 minutes, then remove.

Makes about 16 standard muffins

Pear-Pecan Muffins

1½ cups (12 fl oz/375 ml) water,
  boiling
¼ lb (125 g) dried pears
2 cups (10 oz/315 g) all-purpose
  (plain) flour
2 teaspoons baking powder
½ teaspoon baking soda (bicarbonate
  of soda)
½ teaspoon salt
2 eggs, beaten
¾ cup (6 oz/185 g) sugar
⅓ cup (3 oz/90 g) unsalted butter,
  melted
½ cup (2 oz/60 g) chopped toasted
  pecans
½ cup (1 oz/30 g) chopped candied
  ginger

One of my favorite muffins. It has a delicate crumb, and bits of pear, pecan and candied ginger. Spoon the batter into 6 large muffin cups for delectable giant-sized treats. For a dandy dessert, split the warm muffins and top with fruit and a spoonful of whipped cream.

*I*n a bowl pour the boiling water over the pears. Let stand for 15 minutes. Drain thoroughly, reserving ½ cup (4 fl oz/125 ml) of the liquid. Using a pair of scissors or a sharp knife, cut the pears into ½-inch (12-mm) bits; set aside.

Meanwhile, preheat an oven to 400°F (200°C). Butter standard muffin tins.

In a medium bowl stir and toss together the flour, baking powder, baking soda and salt. Set aside. In a large bowl whisk together the reserved pear-soaking liquid, eggs, sugar and melted butter until smooth. Stir in the pears, pecans and ginger. Add the combined dry ingredients and stir just until blended.

Spoon into the prepared muffin tins, filling each cup about three-quarters full. Bake until a toothpick inserted in the center of a muffin comes out clean, about 20 minutes. Cool in the tins for 5 minutes, then remove.

Makes about 12 standard muffins

Blueberry Muffins

2 cups (10 oz/315 g) all-purpose
  (plain) flour
⅔ cup (5 oz/155 g) sugar
2½ teaspoons baking powder
¼ teaspoon baking soda (bicarbonate
  of soda)
½ teaspoon salt
1 teaspoon ground cinnamon
1 cup (8 fl oz/250 ml) milk
½ cup (4 oz/125 g) unsalted butter,
  melted
2 eggs
1 cup (4 oz/125 g) blueberries

Sweet, buttery and delicately spiced, with a cakelike texture. Fresh blueberries are best, but if you have only frozen berries, stir them into the batter without thawing, or their dark juice will turn the muffins purple.

*P*reheat an oven to 400°F (200°C). Butter standard muffin tins.

In a medium bowl stir and toss together the flour, sugar, baking powder, baking soda, salt and cinnamon. Set aside. In another medium bowl whisk together the milk, butter and eggs until smooth. Add the combined dry ingredients and stir just until blended. Add the blueberries and stir just until evenly incorporated.

Spoon into the prepared muffin tins, filling each cup about three-quarters full. Bake until a toothpick inserted in the center of a muffin comes out clean, 15–20 minutes. Cool in the tins for 5 minutes, then remove.

Makes about 16 standard muffins

Sour Cream–Maple Muffins

1¾ cups (9 oz/280 g) all-purpose (plain) flour
2 teaspoons baking powder
1 teaspoon baking soda (bicarbonate of soda)
½ teaspoon salt
½ cup (4 oz/125 g) unsalted butter, at room temperature
¾ cup (6 fl oz/180 ml) maple syrup
1 cup (8 fl oz/250 ml) sour cream
1 egg
½ cup (2 oz/60 g) chopped pecans

The subtle flavors of butter and sour cream with discreet overtones of maple syrup. A hand-held mixer is useful for blending the butter and syrup, but further mixing is easily done by hand.

❊

Preheat an oven to 400°F (200°C). Butter standard muffin tins.

In a small bowl stir and toss together the flour, baking powder, baking soda and salt. Set aside. In a medium bowl beat the butter until smooth, then slowly add the maple syrup, beating constantly. Beat in the sour cream and egg. Stir in the pecans. Add the combined dry ingredients and stir just until blended.

Spoon into the prepared muffin tins, filling each cup about two-thirds full. Bake until a toothpick inserted in the center of a muffin comes out clean, 15–18 minutes. Cool in the tins for 5 minutes, then remove.

Makes about 16 standard muffins

Peanut Butter Muffins

2 cups (10 oz/315 g) all-purpose (plain) flour

⅓ cup (2½ oz/75 g) firmly packed brown sugar

1 tablespoon baking powder

½ teaspoon salt

⅔ cup (6 oz/185 g) smooth peanut butter

1⅓ cups (11 fl oz/330 ml) milk

¼ cup (2 oz/60 g) unsalted butter, melted

2 eggs

½ cup (3 oz/90 g) chopped roasted peanuts, salted or unsalted

Fine-textured, moist and golden. They aren't too sweet and have a good nutty flavor—you could serve them with a curry or chicken dinner, or with roast pork. For breakfast, pass them with butter, into which you've beaten a little honey.

Preheat an oven to 400°F (200°C). Butter standard muffin tins.

In a large bowl stir and toss together the flour, brown sugar, baking powder and salt. Set aside. In a medium bowl beat the peanut butter briefly until smooth, then beat in a few spoonfuls of the milk. Beat in the remaining milk, then beat in the melted butter and eggs. Stir in the peanuts. Add to the combined dry ingredients and stir just until blended.

Spoon into the prepared muffin tins, filling each cup about three-quarters full. Bake until a toothpick inserted in the center of a muffin comes out clean, about 15 minutes. Cool in the tins for 5 minutes, then remove.

Makes about 16 standard muffins

Triple-Chocolate Muffins

3 squares (3 oz/90 g) unsweetened chocolate

3 squares (3 oz/90 g) semisweet chocolate

¼ cup (2 oz/60 g) unsalted butter

½ cup (2½ oz/75 g) all-purpose (plain) flour

½ teaspoon baking powder

¼ teaspoon salt

2 eggs

½ cup (4 oz/125 g) sugar

1 teaspoon vanilla extract (essence)

1 teaspoon instant coffee granules or powder

½ cup (2 oz/60 g) semisweet chocolate chips

½ cup (2 oz/60 g) chopped walnuts

The chocolate flavor is well-suited to these dense, brownielike muffins, and they are great for packing in lunch boxes or taking on picnics. Take care not to overbake them; they should remain moist in the center.

Preheat an oven to 350°F (180°C). Butter standard muffin tins.

Combine the unsweetened and semisweet chocolates and the butter in the top pan of a double boiler and place over simmering water. Stir frequently until melted and smooth. Set aside to cool slightly.

In a small bowl stir and toss together the flour, baking powder and salt; set aside. In another bowl combine the eggs, sugar, vanilla and coffee granules or powder. Beat until light and about double in volume (a hand-held mixer is useful for this step). Beat in the chocolate mixture and then the combined dry ingredients just until blended. Stir in the chocolate chips and walnuts. The mixture will be stiff, almost like a dough.

Spoon into the prepared muffin tins, filling each cup about two-thirds full. Using moistened fingertips, smooth the top of each muffin. Bake until they look dry on top, about 15 minutes. Do not overbake; the centers should remain moist. Cool in the tins for 10 minutes, then remove.

Makes 12 standard muffins

Poppyseed Muffins

1½ cups (7½ oz/235 g) all-purpose (plain) flour
½ cup (1½ oz/40 g) toasted wheat germ
⅓ cup (3 oz/90 g) poppyseeds
⅓ cup (3 oz/90 g) sugar
1 tablespoon baking powder
½ teaspoon salt
1 cup (8 fl oz/250 ml) milk
1 egg
¼ cup (2 oz/60 g) unsalted butter, melted

Poppyseeds have a subtle but unique flavor—a little earthy and a little spicy at the same time—and they add a nice crunch. Their flavor is complemented by a sweet lemon glaze (recipe on page 12). Wheat germ is usually available toasted, in jars. Roast unprocessed wheat germ in a dry frying pan over medium heat, stirring almost constantly, until lightly browned. If you prefer to omit the wheat germ, increase the amount of flour to 2 cups (10 oz/315 g). If you like, spoon the batter into a half-dozen large muffin cups and serve these giants for breakfast.

Preheat an oven to 400°F (200°C). Butter standard muffin tins.

In a large bowl stir and toss together the flour, wheat germ, poppyseeds, sugar, baking powder and salt. Set aside. In a small bowl whisk together the milk, egg and melted butter until smooth. Add to the dry ingredients and stir just until blended.

Spoon into the prepared muffin tins, filling each cup about two-thirds full. Bake until a toothpick inserted in the center of a muffin comes out clean, 15–18 minutes. Cool in the tins for 3 minutes, then remove.

Makes about 12 standard muffins

Spice Muffins

2 cups (10 oz/315 g) all-purpose (plain) flour

⅔ cup (5 oz/155 g) sugar

1 tablespoon baking powder

½ teaspoon salt

2 teaspoons nutmeg, preferably freshly grated

1 teaspoon ground cinnamon

½ teaspoon ground cloves

½ teaspoon ground allspice

1 egg

1 cup (8 fl oz/250 ml) heavy whipping (double) cream

½ cup (4 fl oz/125 ml) milk

⅓ cup (3 oz/90 g) unsalted butter, melted

¼ cup (1½ oz/45 g) dried currants, optional

Heavy cream gives these a fine, creamy texture and a delicate crumb—and what could be nicer with your morning coffee or afternoon tea.

Preheat an oven to 400°F (200°C). Butter standard muffin tins.

In a large bowl stir and toss together the flour, sugar, baking powder, salt, nutmeg, cinnamon, cloves and allspice. Set aside. In a medium bowl whisk together the egg, cream, milk, melted butter and the currants, if using. Add to the combined dry ingredients and stir just until blended.

Spoon into the prepared muffin tins, filling each cup about two-thirds full. Bake until a toothpick inserted in the center of a muffin comes out clean, about 20 minutes. Cool in the tins for 5 minutes, then remove.

Makes about 12 standard muffins

Boston Brown Bread Muffins

½ cup (2½ oz/75 g) rye flour

½ cup (2½ oz/75 g) yellow cornmeal

½ cup (2½ oz/75 g) whole-wheat
(wholemeal) flour

1½ teaspoons baking soda
(bicarbonate of soda)

¾ teaspoon salt

1 cup (8 fl oz/250 ml) buttermilk

⅓ cup (2½ oz/75 g) firmly packed
dark brown sugar

⅓ cup (3 fl oz/80 ml) vegetable oil

⅓ cup (4 oz/125 g) molasses

1 egg

1 cup (6 oz/185 g) raisins

*From cookbook author Marion Cunningham, these have all
the goodness of—and the same ingredients as—old-fashioned
steamed brown bread, but are much faster to make. Enjoy
them hot from the oven for breakfast, or with baked beans,
coleslaw and fish cakes for a traditional New England supper.*

Preheat an oven to 400°F (200°C). Butter standard
muffin tins.

In a medium bowl stir and toss together the rye flour,
cornmeal, whole-wheat flour, baking soda and salt. Set
aside. In a small bowl whisk together the buttermilk,
sugar, oil, molasses and egg until smooth. Add to the
combined dry ingredients and stir just until blended.
Stir in the raisins.

Spoon into the prepared muffin tins, filling each cup
about two-thirds full. Bake until a toothpick inserted in
the center of a muffin comes out clean, about 15
minutes. Cool in the tins for a moment, then remove.

Makes about 12 standard muffins

Cherry Muffins

½ cup (4 fl oz/125 ml) water, boiling
1 cup (5 oz/155 g) pitted dried
   cherries, coarsely chopped
2 cups (10 oz/315 g) all-purpose
   (plain) flour
2 teaspoons baking powder
1 teaspoon baking soda (bicarbonate
   of soda)
½ teaspoon salt
⅔ cup (5 oz/155 g) sugar
⅓ cup (3 oz/90 g) unsalted butter,
   melted
2 eggs
1 teaspoon finely grated lemon zest
½ teaspoon almond extract (essence)

Dried cherries look like big raisins, and they pack a lot of tart, sweet cherry flavor. You may substitute dried cranberries, if you wish.

Preheat an oven to 375°F (190°C). Butter standard muffin tins.

In a bowl pour the boiling water over the cherries. Let stand for about 5 minutes.

In another bowl stir and toss together the flour, baking powder, baking soda and salt. Set aside. To the cherries and water, add the sugar, melted butter, eggs, lemon zest and almond extract. Add the combined dry ingredients and stir just until blended.

Spoon into the prepared muffin tins, filling each cup about two-thirds full. Bake until a toothpick inserted in the center of a muffin comes out clean, about 20 minutes. Cool in the tins for 5 minutes, then remove.

Makes about 12 standard muffins

Whole-Wheat Pumpkin Bread

2½ cups (12½ oz/390 g) whole-wheat
  (wholemeal) flour
½ cup (2½ oz/75 g) yellow or white
  cornmeal
2 teaspoons baking soda (bicarbonate
  of soda)
1 teaspoon ground ginger
1½ teaspoons ground cinnamon
½ teaspoon ground cloves
½ teaspoon ground nutmeg
½ teaspoon salt
⅔ cup (5 oz/155 g) unsalted butter,
  at room temperature
2 cups (1 lb/500 g) sugar
2 cups (1 lb/500 g) mashed cooked
  pumpkin or canned pumpkin
4 eggs
⅔ cup (5 fl oz/160 ml) water
1 cup (6 oz/185 g) raisins
½ cup (2 oz/60 g) chopped walnuts

*Pumpkin bread is moist, dark and spicy; the cornmeal
gives it an interesting texture. I often make this for holiday
breakfasts, and it makes good sandwiches for holiday
leftovers, too. Whenever it is in the house, I find myself
reaching for more.*

Preheat an oven to 350°F (180°C). Grease and flour
2 medium (8½-inch/21-cm) loaf pans.

In a medium bowl stir and toss together the flour,
cornmeal, baking soda, ginger, cinnamon, cloves,
nutmeg and salt. Set aside. In a large bowl beat together
the butter and sugar until blended; a hand-held mixer
is useful for this step. Beat in the pumpkin, eggs and
water. Add the combined dry ingredients and beat just
until blended. Stir in the raisins and walnuts.

Pour into the 2 prepared pans and bake until a thin
wooden skewer inserted in the center of a loaf comes out
clean, 60–65 minutes. Cool in the pans for 10 minutes,
then turn out onto a wire rack to cool completely.

Makes 2 medium loaves

Fig-Date Bread

1 cup (6 oz/185 g) chopped pitted
    dates
1 cup (5 oz/155 g) chopped dried figs
¼ cup (2 oz/60 g) unsalted butter,
    at room temperature
1½ teaspoons baking soda
    (bicarbonate of soda)
1 cup (8 fl oz/250 ml) water, boiling
½ cup (4 oz/125 g) sugar
½ cup (2 oz/60 g) chopped walnuts
2 eggs
¾ cup (4 oz/125 g) all-purpose (plain)
    flour
¾ cup (4 oz/125 g) whole-wheat
    (wholemeal) flour
½ teaspoon baking powder
½ teaspoon salt

A dark, firm-textured bread with a hearty character. I like to have it for breakfast or with afternoon coffee or tea, thinly sliced and topped with cream cheese and a scattering of chopped dates. You may want to bake this bread in 2 small pans, for smaller slices that are easily eaten out of hand. It keeps well for several days.

In a large bowl combine the dates, figs, butter and baking soda. Pour in the boiling water, stir well and let stand for 15 minutes.

Preheat an oven to 350°F (180°C). Grease and flour a medium (8½-inch/21-cm) loaf pan.

Beat the sugar, walnuts and eggs into the date mixture; set aside. In a medium bowl stir and toss together the all-purpose and whole-wheat flours, baking powder and salt. Add to the date mixture and beat just until blended.

Spread evenly in the prepared pan. Bake until a thin wooden skewer inserted in the center of the loaf comes out clean, 55–65 minutes. Cool in the pan for 10 minutes, then turn out onto a wire rack to cool completely.

Makes 1 medium loaf

Oatmeal-Raisin Bread

1¼ cups (10 fl oz/310 ml) buttermilk

½ cup (1½ oz/45 g) regular uncooked oatmeal (rolled oats)

1½ cups (7½ oz/235 g) all-purpose (plain) flour

1 teaspoon ground cinnamon

1 teaspoon ground ginger

1 teaspoon baking soda (bicarbonate of soda)

1 teaspoon baking powder

½ teaspoon salt

½ cup (4 oz/125 g) sugar

½ cup (4 oz/125 g) unsalted butter, melted

2 eggs

½ cup (3 oz/90 g) raisins

One of the easiest loaves to make—even a child could do it. The bread is golden, cakelike and spicy. If it becomes a little stale, it makes mighty good toast and will taste all the better spruced up with the simple berry jam on page 13.

*I*n a large bowl stir together the buttermilk and oatmeal. Let stand for 30 minutes.

Preheat an oven to 350°F (180°C). Grease and flour a medium (8½-inch/21-cm) loaf pan.

In a small bowl stir and toss together the flour, cinnamon, ginger, baking soda, baking powder and salt. Set aside. Add the sugar, butter, eggs and raisins to the oatmeal mixture and beat until blended. Add the combined dry ingredients and beat just until blended.

Spread evenly in the prepared pan. Bake until a thin wooden skewer inserted in the center of the loaf comes out clean, 55–65 minutes. Cool in the pan for 10 minutes, then turn out onto a wire rack to cool completely.

Makes 1 medium loaf

Lemon Bread

½ cup (4 oz/125 g) vegetable
  shortening
1 cup (8 oz/250 g) sugar
2 eggs
1¼ cups (6½ oz/200 g) all-purpose
  (plain) flour
1 teaspoon baking powder
½ teaspoon salt
½ cup (4 fl oz/125 ml) milk
1 tablespoon finely grated lemon zest
½ cup (2 oz/60 g) chopped pecans

FOR THE LEMON SYRUP:
¼ cup (2 oz/60 g) sugar
3 tablespoons fresh lemon juice

This recipe carries a double dose of lemon: grated zest in the batter and lemon syrup poured over the bread after baking. For a heavenly dessert, bake it in 2 miniature loaf pans, then top the slices with berries and whipped cream.

❉

*P*reheat an oven to 350°F (180°C). Grease and flour a medium (8½-inch/21-cm) loaf pan.

In a large bowl combine the shortening and sugar and beat until blended. Add the eggs, one at a time, beating well after each addition. In a medium bowl stir and toss together the flour, baking powder and salt. Add to the shortening mixture, along with the milk and lemon zest, and beat until blended and smooth. Stir in the pecans. Spread evenly in the prepared pan. Bake until a thin wooden skewer inserted in the center of the loaf comes out clean, about 1 hour.

While the bread bakes, make the lemon syrup by combining the sugar and lemon juice in a small bowl. Set aside, stirring occasionally; don't worry if the sugar does not dissolve completely.

Remove the bread from the oven and, using a fork, gently poke the top in several places. Stir the syrup, then slowly drizzle it over the hot bread. Cool in the pan for 15 minutes, then turn out onto a wire rack to cool completely.

Makes 1 medium loaf

Sour Cream–Raisin Bread

1½ cups (12 fl oz/375 ml) sour cream

1½ teaspoons baking soda
(bicarbonate of soda)

½ cup (4 oz/125 g) unsalted butter,
melted

1 cup (8 oz/250 g) granulated sugar

2 eggs

½ cup (3 oz/90 g) raisins

1¾ cups (9 oz/280 g) all-purpose
(plain) flour

2 teaspoons baking powder

2 teaspoons ground cinnamon

½ teaspoon salt

¼ cup (2 oz/60 g) firmly packed
brown sugar

¼ cup (1 oz/30 g) chopped walnuts

A sweet, spicy brown sugar topping crowns this rich bread. For an even more delectable treat, top it with cinnamon-laced whipped cream. Good for a special Sunday brunch—or whenever you want to splurge—and it keeps well, too.

❈

Preheat an oven to 350°F (180°C). Grease and flour a large (9-inch/23-cm) loaf pan.

In a large bowl stir together the sour cream and baking soda. Set aside for 5 minutes. Add the melted butter, granulated sugar, eggs and raisins and whisk until blended. Set aside.

In a small bowl stir and toss together the flour, baking powder, 1 teaspoon of the cinnamon and the salt. Add to the sour cream mixture and stir just until blended.

Spread evenly in the prepared pan. Stir together the remaining 1 teaspoon cinnamon, the brown sugar and walnuts. Sprinkle over the batter. Bake until a thin wooden skewer inserted in the center of the loaf comes out clean, 65–75 minutes. Cool in the pan for 15 minutes, then turn out onto a wire rack to cool completely.

Makes 1 large loaf

Whole-Wheat Banana Nut Bread

2½ cups (12½ oz/390 g) whole-wheat (wholemeal) flour

2 teaspoons baking soda (bicarbonate of soda)

1 teaspoon salt

1 cup (8 oz/250 g) unsalted butter, at room temperature

2 cups (1 lb/500 g) sugar

2 cups (1 lb/500 g) mashed ripe banana (4 large bananas)

4 eggs

1 cup (4 oz/125 g) chopped walnuts or pecans

Dark, rich and sweet. A slice of this bread is good for breakfast, toasted and spread with softened cream cheese.

Preheat an oven to 350°F (180°C). Grease and flour 2 medium (8½-inch/21-cm) loaf pans.

In a medium bowl stir and toss together the flour, baking soda and salt. Set aside. In a large bowl beat together the butter and sugar until blended; a hand-held mixer is useful for this step. Beat in the banana, then beat in the eggs until completely mixed; don't worry if the mixture looks curdled—this is only because of the moisture in the mixture, and is not a flaw. Stir in the nuts. Add the combined dry ingredients and stir just until blended.

Spread evenly in the 2 prepared pans. Bake until a thin wooden skewer inserted in the center of a loaf comes out clean, 55–65 minutes. Cool in the pans for 10 minutes, then turn out onto a wire rack to cool completely.

Makes 2 medium loaves

Patsy's Honey-Nut Bread

1 cup (8 fl oz/250 ml) milk

1 cup (12 oz/375 g) honey

½ cup (4 oz/125 g) sugar

2½ cups (12½ oz/390 g) all-purpose (plain) flour

1 teaspoon baking soda (bicarbonate of soda)

1 teaspoon salt

¼ cup (2 oz/60 g) unsalted butter, melted

2 egg yolks

½ cup (2 oz/60 g) chopped walnuts

Dense, moist and golden, this is a fine recipe from a wonderful San Francisco cook and friend, Patsy McFetridge. Serve it with fruit salads and compotes, or with a bowl of yogurt for breakfast; the bread is even better the day after it is baked. Spread it with honey-swirled butter. It is good to have on hand for holidays and, if you wish, bake it in a springform pan rather than the traditional loaf pan.

Preheat an oven to 325°F (165°C). Grease and flour a large (9-inch/23-cm) loaf pan or a 7-inch (18-cm) springform pan.

In a medium saucepan bring the milk to a simmer over medium heat. Add the honey and sugar and stir until the sugar dissolves. Set aside to cool to tepid.

Meanwhile, in a medium bowl stir and toss together the flour, baking soda and salt. Set aside. Add the melted butter and egg yolks to the cooled honey mixture and whisk until blended. Add to the combined dry ingredients and beat until thoroughly blended. Stir in the walnuts.

Spread evenly in the prepared pan. Bake until a thin wooden skewer inserted in the center of the loaf comes out clean, 60–70 minutes. Cool in the pan for 15 minutes, then turn out onto a wire rack to cool completely.

Makes 1 large loaf

Holiday Fruit Bread

1¾ cups (9 oz/280 g) all-purpose (plain) flour

½ cup (4 oz/125 g) sugar

1 tablespoon baking powder

½ teaspoon salt

¾ cup (6 fl oz/180 ml) milk

2 eggs

⅓ cup (3 oz/90 g) unsalted butter, melted

¾ cup (4½ oz/140 g) finely chopped dried apricots

¾ cup (4½ oz/140 g) finely chopped pitted prunes

½ cup (2 oz/60 g) chopped walnuts or almonds

A moist bread, with so much flavor and texture that it would make a respectable holiday fruit cake. It is chockful of fruit and nuts, and remains fresh-tasting for several days. If you want a round loaf rather than the conventional shape, bake the batter in a springform pan and decorate the top with dried fruit.

Preheat an oven to 350°F (180°C). Grease and flour a medium (8½-inch/21-cm) loaf pan or a 7-inch (18-cm) springform pan.

In a large bowl stir and toss together the flour, sugar, baking powder and salt. Set aside. In a medium bowl whisk together the milk, eggs and melted butter until smooth. Stir in the apricots, prunes and nuts. Add to the combined dry ingredients and stir just until blended.

Spread evenly in the prepared pan. Bake until a thin wooden skewer inserted in the center of the loaf comes out clean, 55–65 minutes. Cool in the pan for 10 minutes, then turn out onto a wire rack to cool completely.

Makes 1 medium loaf

Buttermilk-Bacon Muffins

6 slices bacon

2 cups (10 oz/315 g) all-purpose (plain) flour

2 tablespoons sugar

2 teaspoons baking powder

½ teaspoon baking soda (bicarbonate of soda)

½ teaspoon salt

1 cup (8 fl oz/250 ml) buttermilk

⅓ cup (3 fl oz/80 ml) corn oil

1 egg

1 small Golden Delicious apple, peeled, cored and finely chopped

Apples and smoky bacon are a wonderful combination anytime, and they make a good-tasting muffin, too. Serve these for breakfast with fried or scrambled eggs or with a bowl of hot cereal. Store any leftover muffins in the refrigerator.

Preheat an oven to 400°F (200°C). Butter standard muffin tins.

In a frying pan, fry the bacon until crisp. Remove to paper towels to drain and cool. Crumble the cooled bacon and set aside.

In a medium bowl, stir and toss together the flour, sugar, baking powder, baking soda and salt. Set aside. In a small bowl whisk together the buttermilk, oil and egg until smooth. Add to the combined dry ingredients, along with the apple and the reserved bacon, and stir just until blended.

Spoon into the prepared muffin tins, filling each cup about three-quarters full. Bake until a toothpick inserted in the center of a muffin comes out clean, about 20 minutes. Cool in the tins for 3 minutes, then remove.

Makes about 12 standard muffins

Cornmeal Nugget Muffins

1 cup (8 fl oz/250 ml) water, boiling
½ cup (2½ oz/75 g) yellow cornmeal
1 teaspoon salt
2 cups (10 oz/315 g) all-purpose
  (plain) flour
3 tablespoons sugar
2 teaspoons baking powder
½ teaspoon baking soda (bicarbonate
  of soda)
1 cup (8 fl oz/250 ml) buttermilk
1 egg
⅓ cup (3 oz/90 g) unsalted butter,
  melted

Small nuggets of toasted cornmeal give these buttery corn muffins the appearance of containing tiny golden pebbles. Serve them with any lively soup, stew or chili.

Preheat an oven to 375°F (190°C). Butter standard muffin tins and a baking sheet.

In a small bowl stir together the boiling water, cornmeal and ½ teaspoon of the salt; don't worry if some small lumps remain in the mixture. Spread in a thin layer on the prepared baking sheet and place in the oven until golden brown and toasted looking, about 25 minutes. Cool completely, then crumble into small pieces. Set aside.

In a medium bowl stir and toss together the flour, sugar, baking powder, baking soda and the remaining ½ teaspoon salt. Set aside. In a small bowl whisk together the buttermilk, egg and melted butter until smooth. Add to the combined dry ingredients, along with the cornmeal nuggets, and stir just until blended.

Spoon into the prepared muffin tins, filling each cup about three-quarters full. Bake until a toothpick inserted in the center of a muffin comes out clean, about 20 minutes. Cool in the tins for 3 minutes, then remove.

Makes about 12 standard muffins

Apple-Cheddar Muffins

1 large apple, such as a Golden
  Delicious or pippin

1½ cups (7½ oz/235 g) all-purpose
  (plain) flour

¼ cup (¾ oz/20 g) regular uncooked
  oatmeal (rolled oats)

2 tablespoons sugar

2 teaspoons baking powder

½ teaspoon baking soda (bicarbonate
  of soda)

½ teaspoon salt

¾ cup (6 fl oz/180 ml) milk

2 eggs

¼ cup (2 oz/60 g) unsalted butter,
  melted

¾ cup (3 oz/90 g) finely grated
  Cheddar cheese

Moist and gutsy, and especially delicious with pork, duck or chicken. They also travel well, making them good lunch box and picnic fare.

Preheat an oven to 400°F (200°C). Butter standard muffin tins.

Peel, halve and core the apple. Cut it into ⅛-inch (3-mm) dice; set aside.

In a large bowl stir and toss together the flour, oatmeal, sugar, baking powder, baking soda and salt. Set aside. In a medium bowl whisk together the milk, eggs and melted butter until smooth. Stir in the apple and cheese. Add to the combined dry ingredients and stir just until blended.

Spoon into the prepared muffin tins, filling each cup about three-quarters full. Bake until a toothpick inserted in the center of a muffin comes out clean, about 20 minutes. Cool in the tins for 3 minutes, then remove.

Makes about 12 standard muffins

Corn Kernel–Bacon Muffins

6 slices bacon

1 cup (5 oz/155 g) all-purpose (plain) flour

1 cup (5 oz/155 g) yellow or white cornmeal

3 tablespoons sugar

1 tablespoon baking powder

½ teaspoon salt

1 cup (8 fl oz/250 ml) milk

1 egg

½ cup (3 oz/90 g) fresh corn kernels or thawed frozen corn kernels

A little crisp bacon gives these muffins a hearty flavor, while cornmeal and corn kernels lend an earthy texture. You may, if you wish, substitute vegetable oil for the bacon drippings, although the bacon taste will be slightly diminished. Keep any leftovers in the refrigerator.

*P*reheat an oven to 400°F (200°C). Butter standard muffin tins.

In a frying pan fry the bacon until crisp. Remove to paper towels to drain and cool. Reserve ¼ cup (2 fl oz/60 ml) of the drippings. Crumble the cooled bacon and set aside.

In a medium bowl stir and toss together the flour, cornmeal, sugar, baking powder and salt. Set aside. In a small bowl whisk together the milk, egg, corn kernels and reserved bacon drippings until blended. Add to the combined dry ingredients, along with the crumbled bacon, and stir just until blended.

Spoon into the prepared muffin tins, filling each cup about two-thirds full. Bake until a toothpick inserted in the center of a muffin comes out clean, about 15 minutes. Cool in the tins for 3 minutes, then remove.

Makes about 16 standard muffins

Chili-Corn Muffins

¾ cup (4 oz/125 g) all-purpose (plain) flour

¾ cup (4 oz/125 g) yellow or white cornmeal

2 teaspoons baking powder

½ teaspoon baking soda (bicarbonate of soda)

½ teaspoon salt

1½ teaspoons chili powder

¾ cup (6 fl oz/180 ml) sour cream

2 eggs

¼ cup (2 oz/60 g) unsalted butter, melted

¼ cup (1½ oz/45 g) diced, peeled green chilies

½ cup (2 oz/60 g) finely grated Cheddar cheese

Moist and rich, these are perfection when warm from the oven and spread with lots of butter. For a casual supper or a lively brunch, serve them with huevos rancheros. Green chilies are available in cans, already roasted, peeled and diced—a great convenience.

Preheat an oven to 400°F (200°C). Butter standard muffin tins.

In a large bowl stir and toss together the flour, cornmeal, baking powder, baking soda, salt and chili powder. Set aside. In a medium bowl whisk together the sour cream, eggs and melted butter until smooth. Stir in the chilies and cheese. Add to the dry ingredients and stir just until blended.

Spoon into the prepared muffin tins, filling each cup about two-thirds full. Bake until a toothpick inserted in the center of a muffin comes out clean, about 15 minutes. Cool in the tins for 3 minutes, then remove.

Makes about 12 standard muffins

Sun-Dried Tomato–Herb Muffins

2 cups (10 oz/315 g) all-purpose (plain) flour

1 tablespoon baking powder

½ teaspoon salt

¼ teaspoon freshly ground pepper

1 cup (8 fl oz/250 ml) milk

1 egg

¼ cup (2 fl oz/60 ml) olive oil

½ cup (2 oz/60 g) freshly grated Parmesan cheese

¼ cup (2 oz/60 g) finely chopped sun-dried tomatoes

2 teaspoons chopped fresh thyme, oregano or dill, or 1 teaspoon dried herb

These muffins, with their Italian accent, are perfect partners to luncheon soups and salads. Flecked with red and green, they are full of tomato and cheese flavor. Buy sun-dried tomatoes that have been packed in olive oil; drain well before using.

Preheat an oven to 375°F (190°C). Butter standard muffin tins.

In a large bowl stir and toss together the flour, baking powder, salt and pepper. Set aside. In a medium bowl whisk together the milk, egg and oil until smooth. Add the cheese, tomatoes and herb and stir until blended. Add to the combined dry ingredients and stir just until blended.

Spoon into the prepared muffin tins, filling each cup about three-quarters full. Bake until a toothpick inserted in the center of a muffin comes out clean, about 20 minutes. Cool in the tins for 3 minutes, then remove.

Makes about 12 standard muffins

Potato Muffins

1 cup (5 oz/155 g) all-purpose (plain) flour

1 cup (4 oz/125 g) potato starch (potato flour)

1 tablespoon sugar

1 tablespoon baking powder

½ teaspoon salt

1½ teaspoons chopped fresh thyme or ½ teaspoon dried thyme

1 cup (8 fl oz/250 ml) milk

½ cup (4 oz/125 g) warm mashed potatoes

1 egg

¼ cup (2 oz/60 g) unsalted butter, melted

⅓ cup (1½ oz/45 g) finely grated Swiss or Cheddar cheese

Potato starch produces breads that are slightly chewy and have a subtle potato flavor. These muffins are wonderful for lunch with a green salad and cheese, or with any chicken dish. Or bake the batter in about 30 miniature muffin cups for placing out on the buffet table. Let them cool for about 10 minutes before serving—they are best just slightly warm or at room temperature. A flavorful caper-mustard butter (recipe on page 15) provides a nice contrast to the delicate muffins.

Preheat an oven to 400°F (200°C). Butter standard muffin tins.

In a large bowl stir and toss together the flour, potato starch, sugar, baking powder, salt and thyme. Set aside. In a medium bowl whisk together the milk and mashed potatoes, then add the egg, melted butter and cheese and whisk until well mixed. Add to the combined dry ingredients and stir just until blended.

Spoon into the prepared muffin tins, filling each cup about three-quarters full. Bake until a toothpick inserted in the center of a muffin comes out clean, 15–18 minutes. Cool in the tins for 3 minutes, then remove.

Makes about 12 standard muffins

Cottage Cheese Muffins

2 cups (10 oz/315 g) all-purpose
  (plain) flour
1 tablespoon sugar
2½ teaspoons baking powder
½ teaspoon baking soda (bicarbonate
  of soda)
½ teaspoon salt
1 egg
1 cup (8 fl oz/250 ml) milk
¼ cup (2 oz/60 g) unsalted butter,
  melted
1 tablespoon chopped fresh dill or
  sage, or 1 teaspoon dried dill or sage
¾ cup (6 oz/185 g) small-curd cottage
  cheese

*Cottage cheese imparts a definite tang to these muffins. They
are quite substantial, and good with a platter of grilled
vegetables or a vegetable casserole for a vegetarian meal.*

Preheat an oven to 375°F (190°C). Butter standard
muffin tins.

In a medium bowl stir and toss together the flour,
sugar, baking powder, baking soda and salt. Set aside.
In another medium bowl whisk together the egg, milk,
melted butter and herb until smooth. Add the cottage
cheese and whisk until blended. Add to the combined
dry ingredients and stir just until blended.

Spoon into the prepared muffin tins, filling each cup
about three-quarters full. Bake until a toothpick inserted
in the center of a muffin comes out clean, about 20
minutes. Cool in the tins for 3 minutes, then remove.

Makes about 16 standard muffins

Nine-Grain Bread

¾ cup (6 fl oz/180 ml) water, boiling

½ cup (3 oz/90 g) 9-grain cereal

1¾ cups (9 oz/280 g) whole-wheat (wholemeal) flour

½ cup (2 oz/60 g) cake (soft-wheat) flour

2 teaspoons baking powder

1 teaspoon baking soda (bicarbonate of soda)

1 teaspoon salt

1½ cups (12 fl oz/375 ml) buttermilk

⅓ cup (4 oz/125 g) honey

⅓ cup (3 fl oz/80 ml) vegetable oil

1 egg

Nine-grain cereal usually contains cracked rye, barley, rice, corn, oats, millet, flax, soy and triticale. It is coarse and earthy and often valued for its fiber and nutrients. Look for it in health-food stores, and enjoy the crunchy texture and the taste of grain it imparts to this simple bread.

In a small bowl pour the boiling water over the cereal and stir well. Let stand for 20 minutes, then drain off any remaining water.

Meanwhile, preheat an oven to 350°F (180°C). Grease and flour a large (9-inch/23-cm) loaf pan.

In a large bowl stir and toss together the whole-wheat flour, cake flour, baking powder, baking soda and salt. Set aside. In another bowl whisk together the buttermilk, honey, oil and egg until smooth. Stir in the cereal. Add to the combined dry ingredients and stir just until blended.

Spread in the prepared pan. Bake until a thin wooden skewer inserted in the center of the loaf comes out clean, 55–60 minutes. Cool in the pan for 10 minutes, then turn out onto a wire rack to cool completely.

Makes 1 large loaf

Nutted Squash Bread

2 cups (10 oz/315 g) all-purpose
(plain) flour

2 teaspoons baking powder

¼ teaspoon baking soda (bicarbonate
of soda)

½ teaspoon salt

½ teaspoon ground nutmeg

1 cup (8 oz/250 g) mashed cooked
winter squash

⅓ cup (3 fl oz/80 ml) milk

⅓ cup (3 oz/90 g) unsalted butter,
melted

2 eggs

¼ cup (2 oz/60 g) firmly packed
brown sugar

½ teaspoon vanilla extract (essence)

½ cup (2 oz/60 g) chopped toasted
walnuts or pecans

¼ cup (1½ oz/45 g) raisins

Golden and fine textured, this bread rises to great heights. It is just slightly sweet and has a cold-weather quality. Serve it with hearty soups and stews, or with baked beans in place of traditional steamed brown bread. Use any mashed, cooked winter squash in the batter, such as acorn, Hubbard, butternut, or even cooked or canned pumpkin.

Preheat an oven to 350°F (180°C). Grease and flour a medium (8½-inch/21-cm) loaf pan.

In a medium bowl stir and toss together the flour, baking powder, baking soda, salt and nutmeg. Set aside. In another medium bowl, whisk together the squash, milk, melted butter, eggs, brown sugar and vanilla until smooth. Stir in the nuts and raisins. Add to the combined dry ingredients and stir just until blended.

Spread evenly in the prepared pan. Bake until a thin wooden skewer inserted in the center of the loaf comes out clean, 60–65 minutes. Cool in the pan for 10 minutes, then turn out onto a wire rack to cool completely.

Makes 1 medium loaf

Whole-Wheat Walnut Bread

1½ cups (7½ oz/235 g) whole-wheat (wholemeal) flour

1 cup (5 oz/155 g) all-purpose (plain) flour

1 teaspoon baking powder

1 teaspoon baking soda (bicarbonate of soda)

½ teaspoon salt

1½ cups (12 fl oz/375 ml) buttermilk

⅓ cup (3 fl oz/80 ml) vegetable oil

⅓ cup (4 oz/125 g) molasses

1 cup (4 oz/125 g) chopped toasted walnuts

Dark and dense with a wheaty flavor and the crunch of walnuts. Serve this eggless bread with hearty soups and stews, main course salads, or fruit and cheese. A very good bread for so little effort, and it makes nice breakfast toast, too.

Preheat an oven to 350°F (180°C). Grease and flour a large (9-inch/23-cm) loaf pan.

In a large bowl stir and toss together the whole-wheat flour, all-purpose flour, baking powder, baking soda and salt. Set aside. In a medium bowl whisk together the buttermilk, oil and molasses until smooth. Stir in the walnuts. Add to the combined dry ingredients and stir just until blended.

Spread evenly in the prepared pan. Bake until a thin wooden skewer inserted in the center of the loaf comes out clean, about 55 minutes. Cool in the pan for 10 minutes, then turn out onto a wire rack to cool completely.

Makes 1 large loaf

Vegetable-Nut Bread

1 cup (5 oz/155 g) whole-wheat (wholemeal) flour

1 cup (5 oz/155 g) all-purpose (plain) flour

1 tablespoon baking powder

¼ teaspoon baking soda (bicarbonate of soda)

½ teaspoon ground ginger

1 teaspoon salt

1 cup (8 fl oz/250 ml) milk

3 tablespoons honey

3 tablespoons olive oil

1 egg

½ cup (3½ oz/105 g) chopped cooked spinach, thoroughly drained

½ cup (2 oz/60 g) chopped toasted walnuts or almonds

½ cup (2 oz/60 g) freshly grated Parmesan or Swiss cheese

A green-flecked, flavorful bread loaded with many good things. It is hearty and healthful—an ideal companion to vegetarian meals. You can use other chopped cooked vegetables instead of spinach, and vary the cheese as well. This bread does not keep, so wrap and freeze what you will not use within a day.

Preheat an oven to 375°F (190°C). Grease and flour a medium (8½-inch/21-cm) loaf pan.

In a large bowl stir and toss together the whole-wheat flour, all-purpose flour, baking powder, baking soda, ginger and salt. Set aside. In a medium bowl whisk together the milk, honey, oil and egg. Stir in the spinach, nuts and cheese. Add to the combined dry ingredients and stir just until blended.

Spread evenly in the prepared pan. Bake until a thin wooden skewer inserted in the center of the loaf comes out clean, 50–55 minutes. Cool in the pan for 10 minutes, then turn out onto a wire rack to cool completely.

Makes 1 medium loaf

Pistachio-Olive Bread

1½ cups (7½ oz/235 g) all-purpose (plain) flour

1 tablespoon sugar

2½ teaspoons baking powder

½ teaspoon salt

¾ cup (6 fl oz/180 ml) milk

¼ cup (2 fl oz/60 ml) olive oil

2 eggs

⅓ cup (1½ oz/45 g) chopped pistachios

3 tablespoons chopped pitted Greek olives

Pistachios, black olives and olive oil give this bread flecks of color and an enticing flavor and aroma. Tender and cakelike, it goes especially well with omelets and other egg dishes. Greek olives, by the way, are pungent and quite salty, so a few go a long way. Cut the flesh from the pit with a small, sharp knife, then chop it finely. Other cured olives may be used as well.

Preheat an oven to 350°F (180°C). Grease and flour a medium (8½-inch/21-cm) loaf pan.

In a medium bowl stir and toss together the flour, sugar, baking powder and salt. Set aside. In a small bowl whisk together the milk, oil and eggs until smooth. Stir in the pistachios and olives. Add to the combined dry ingredients and stir just until blended.

Spread evenly in the prepared pan. Bake until a thin wooden skewer inserted in the center of the loaf comes out clean, about 50 minutes. Cool in the pan for 10 minutes, then turn out onto a wire rack to cool completely.

Makes 1 medium loaf

Oat Flour Bread

1 cup (5 oz/155 g) all-purpose (plain) flour

1 cup (4 oz/125 g) oat flour

¼ cup (2 oz/60 g) firmly packed brown sugar

2 teaspoons baking powder

½ teaspoon baking soda (bicarbonate of soda)

½ teaspoon salt

1 cup (8 fl oz/250 ml) buttermilk

1 egg

¼ cup (2 fl oz/60 ml) olive oil

¼ cup (1½ oz/45 g) raisins

¼ cup (1 oz/30 g) chopped walnuts or almonds

Oat flour is simply whole oats ground to a powder, and it is even sometimes labeled "oatmeal flour." It lends this bread the subtle taste of oatmeal, as well as a sturdy, chewy character. The loaf is crumbly when warm, and will cut more easily at room temperature. A piece of this bread and some fruit are a wonderful way to begin the day; for a special breakfast, I like this toasted and spread with applesauce or pear preserves (see recipe for pear-ginger jam on page 13).

Preheat an oven to 375°F (190°C). Grease and flour a medium (8½-inch/21-cm) loaf pan.

In a medium bowl stir and toss together the all-purpose flour, oat flour, brown sugar, baking powder, baking soda and salt. Set aside. In a small bowl whisk together the buttermilk, egg and olive oil until smooth. Stir in the raisins and nuts. Add to the combined dry ingredients and stir just until blended.

Spread evenly in the prepared pan. Bake until a thin wooden skewer inserted in the center of the bread comes out clean, about 50 minutes. Cool in the pan for 10 minutes, then turn out onto a wire rack to cool completely.

Makes 1 medium loaf

Whole-Wheat Bulgur Bread

½ cup (3 oz/90 g) bulgur

¾ cup (6 fl oz/180 ml) water, boiling

1½ cups (7½ oz/235 g) whole-wheat (wholemeal) flour

½ cup (2½ oz/75 g) all-purpose (plain) flour

1 tablespoon baking powder

1 teaspoon salt

¼ cup (2 oz/60 g) firmly packed brown sugar

1½ cups (12 fl oz/375 ml) milk

2 eggs

⅓ cup (3 oz/80 g) vegetable shortening, melted

½ cup (2 oz/60 g) chopped toasted pecans

Bulgur is cracked wheat, and although the bits are quite hard and crunchy, soaking them briefly softens them. It adds a unique character and flavor to this whole-wheat loaf. This bread will keep for several days and is especially good served with a platter of sliced tomatoes, dressed with olive oil and lemon and garnished with feta cheese. Round out the menu with some tomato-basil butter (recipe on page 15)—it's good on crackers, too—and you will have an outstanding summertime luncheon.

In a small bowl stir together the bulgur and boiling water. Let stand for 30 minutes, then fluff the grains with a fork.

Meanwhile, preheat an oven to 350°F (180°C). Grease and flour a large (9-inch/23-cm) loaf pan.

In a medium bowl stir and toss together the whole-wheat flour, all-purpose flour, baking powder, salt and brown sugar. Set aside. In another medium bowl whisk together the milk, eggs and melted shortening until smooth. Stir in the bulgur and pecans. Add to the combined dry ingredients and stir just until blended.

Spread evenly in the prepared pan. Bake until a thin wooden skewer inserted in the center of the loaf comes out clean, about 1 hour. Cool in the pan for 10 minutes, then turn out onto a wire rack to cool completely.

Makes 1 large loaf

Buckwheat Kasha Bread

¼ cup (2 oz/50 g) kasha

⅓ cup (3 fl oz/80 ml) water, boiling

1 cup (4 oz/125 g) buckwheat flour

1 cup (5 oz/155 g) all-purpose (plain) flour

⅓ cup (2 oz/60 g) firmly packed brown sugar

1 teaspoon baking powder

1 teaspoon baking soda (bicarbonate of soda)

½ teaspoon salt

1 cup (8 fl oz/250 ml) buttermilk

1 egg

¼ cup (2 fl oz/60 ml) vegetable oil or olive oil

½ cup (2 oz/60 g) chopped hazelnuts (filberts) or walnuts

Buckwheat flour (which is actually not related to wheat at all) is used frequently in pancakes and yeast breads, imparting a dark, earthy character and a unique, claylike aroma. Kasha, roasted buckwheat groats, is milled from the same seed as the flour, but is more coarsely ground. This dark bread has a distinctive character that excels with hearty winter dishes.

*I*n a small bowl stir together the kasha and boiling water. Let stand for 15 minutes.

Preheat an oven to 350°F (180°C). Grease and flour a medium (8½-inch/21-cm) loaf pan.

In a large bowl stir and toss together the buckwheat flour, all-purpose flour, brown sugar, baking powder, baking soda and salt. Set aside. In a small bowl whisk together the buttermilk, egg and oil until smooth. Stir in the nuts and the kasha mixture. Add to the combined dry ingredients and stir just until blended.

Spread evenly in the prepared pan. Bake until a thin wooden skewer inserted in the center of the loaf comes out clean, about 1 hour. Cool in the pan for 10 minutes, then turn out onto a wire rack to cool completely.

Makes 1 medium loaf

Cheese-and-Grits Bread

1 cup (5 oz/155 g) all-purpose (plain) flour

1 cup (6 oz/185 g) quick-cooking hominy grits

1 tablespoon sugar

2 teaspoons chopped fresh rosemary or 1 teaspoon crumbled dried rosemary

1 teaspoon baking soda (bicarbonate of soda)

½ teaspoon salt

1½ cups (12 fl oz/375 ml) buttermilk

1 egg

⅓ cup (3 oz/90 g) unsalted butter, melted

1 cup (4 oz/125 g) finely grated Cheddar or Swiss cheese, or a mixture

Hominy grits are made from dried, ground corn kernels that have had the hull and germ removed. Grits look like coarse cornmeal and are frequently eaten in the southern United States. They are widely available elsewhere, however, and anyone will appreciate their comforting down-home flavor. This rough-hewn bread, scented with rosemary, is best warm from the oven, spread with butter.

Preheat an oven to 400°F (200°C). Butter an 8-inch (20-cm) square pan.

In a large bowl stir and toss together the flour, grits, sugar, rosemary, baking soda and salt. Set aside. In a medium bowl whisk together the buttermilk, egg and melted butter until smooth. Stir in the cheese. Add to the combined dry ingredients and stir just until blended.

Spread in the prepared pan. Bake until a toothpick inserted in the center of the bread comes out clean, 25–30 minutes. Cut into 2-inch (5-cm) squares and serve warm from the pan.

Makes 16 squares

Herbed Cheese-Beer Bread

2½ cups (12½ oz/390 g) all-purpose (plain) flour
2 tablespoons sugar
1 tablespoon baking powder
1½ teaspoons baking soda (bicarbonate of soda)
1 teaspoon salt
1 tablespoon chopped fresh sage or 1½ teaspoons dried sage
1½ cups (12 fl oz/375 ml) beer, freshly opened
1 cup (4 oz/125 g) finely grated Cheddar cheese

Beer gives bread a yeasty flavor and aroma, even when there is no yeast in it. With no milk or eggs, this is also one of the easiest loaves to make. It is good with all manner of soups and salads, and thinly sliced, makes great ham and cheese sandwiches.

❈

Preheat an oven to 375°F (190°C). Grease and flour a large (9-inch/23-cm) loaf pan.

In a medium bowl stir and toss together the flour, sugar, baking powder, baking soda, salt and sage. Stir in the beer and cheese until completely blended.

Spread evenly in the prepared pan. Bake until a thin wooden skewer inserted in the center of the loaf comes out clean, 50–55 minutes. Cool in the pan for 10 minutes, then turn out onto a wire rack to cool completely.

Makes 1 large loaf

Glossary

The following glossary defines terms specifically as they relate to sweet and savory muffins and quick breads. Included are major and unusual ingredients and basic techniques.

ACORN SQUASH
See winter squash.

ALLSPICE
Sweet spice of Caribbean origin with a flavor suggesting a blend of **cinnamon, cloves** and **nutmeg,** hence its name. May be purchased as whole dried berries or ground.

ALMOND EXTRACT
Flavoring derived by dissolving the essential oil of almonds in an alcohol base. Use only products labeled "pure" or "natural" almond extract (essence).

ALMONDS
See nuts.

BAKING POWDER
Commercial baking product combining three ingredients: **baking soda,** the source of the carbon dioxide gas that causes muffins and quick breads to rise; an acid such as **cream of tartar,** calcium acid phosphate or sodium aluminum sulphate, which, when the powder is combined with a liquid, causes the baking soda to release its gas; and a starch, such as cornstarch or flour, to keep the powder resistant to moisture.

BAKING SODA
Also known as bicarbonate of soda or sodium bicarbonate, the active component of **baking powder** and the source of the carbon dioxide gas that leavens muffins and quick breads. Often used on its own to leaven batters that include acidic ingredients such as **buttermilk,** yogurt or citrus juices.

BASIL
Sweet, spicy herb popular in Italian and French cooking, particularly with tomatoes.

BRAN
The papery brown coating of a whole grain, usually removed during milling. Unless the type of grain is specified, the term usually refers to wheat bran. Included in batter mixtures, it provides robust flavor and texture, as well as a generous measure of dietary fiber. Oat and rice brans are also popular sources. Found in the baking or breakfast cereal section of the supermarket.

BULGUR
Wheat berries (below, right) that have been washed, parboiled, dried, partially debranned and cracked into coarse particles (left) that contribute a nutlike taste and chewy texture to muffins and quick breads. Sold in shops specializing in Middle Eastern foods, in health-food stores and in well-stocked supermarkets. Also known as burghul.

BUTTERMILK
Form of cultured low-fat or nonfat milk that contributes a tangy flavor and thick, creamy texture to muffins and quick breads. Its acidity also provides a boost to leavening agents, adding extra lightness to batters.

BUTTERNUT SQUASH
See winter squash.

CAPERS
Small, pickled buds of a bush common to the Mediterranean; used as a savory flavoring or garnish.

CHEDDAR CHEESE
Firm, smooth-textured whole-milk cheese, pale yellow-white to deep yellow-orange and ranging in taste from mild and sweet when fresh to rich and sharply tangy when aged.

CHILI PEPPER, GREEN
The unripened form of any of a wide variety of fresh peppers prized for the mild-to-hot spiciness they impart as a seasoning. They include the mild-to-hot, dark green poblano; the long, mild Anaheim; and the small, fiery jalapeño. When handling any chili, wear kitchen gloves to prevent any cuts or abrasions on your hands from contacting the pepper's volatile oils; wash your hands well with warm, soapy water, and take special care not to touch your eyes or any other sensitive areas.

CHILI POWDER
Commercial blend of spices featuring ground dried chili peppers along with such other seasonings as cumin, **oregano, cloves,** coriander, pepper and salt. Best purchased in small quantities, because flavor diminishes rapidly after opening.

CHOCOLATE
Purchase the best-quality baking chocolate you can find, including unsweetened, bittersweet, semisweet or sweet type, as the recipe requires. Care must be taken to melt chocolate without scorching. A double boiler, in which the chocolate melts above water kept below a simmer, ensures gentle heat.

CINNAMON
Popular sweet spice for flavoring baked goods. The aromatic bark of a type of evergreen tree, it is sold as whole dried strips—cinnamon sticks—or ground.

CLOVE
Rich and aromatic East African spice used in its ground form to flavor muffin batters.

CORNMEAL
Granular flour ground from dried kernels of yellow or white corn, with a sweet, robust flavor that is particularly appealing in baked goods. Commercial cornmeal, sold in supermarkets, lacks the kernel's husk and germ and is available in fine or coarser grinds; stone-ground cornmeal, made from whole corn kernels, produces a richer flour better suited to cornbread.

CREAM, HEAVY WHIPPING
Cream with a high butterfat content—at least 36 percent—that adds richness to muffins. Also called double cream.

CREAM, SOUR
Commercial dairy product made from pasteurized sweet cream, used to add richness and tang to baked goods. Like **buttermilk**, its extra acidity boosts the leavening action of **baking soda**.

DRIED FRUIT
Intensely flavored and satisfyingly chewy, many forms of sun-dried or kiln-dried fruits may be added to enhance the taste or texture of muffins and quick breads. Select more recently dried and packaged fruits, which have a softer texture than older dried fruits. Usually found in specialty-food shops or supermarket baking sections. Some of the most popular options include:

Apricots
Pitted whole or halved fruits, sweet and slightly tangy.

Cherries
Ripe tart red cherries that have been pitted and dried—usually in a kiln, with a little sugar added to help preserve them—to a consistency and shape resembling that of raisins.

Currants
Produced from a small variety of grapes, these dried fruits resemble tiny raisins but have a stronger, tarter flavor. If unavailable, substitute raisins.

CREAM OF TARTAR
Acidic powder extracted during wine making that is used as a leavening agent, most commonly combined with **baking soda** to make commercial **baking powder**.

Figs
Compact form (below) of the succulent black or golden summertime fruit, distinguished by a slightly crunchy texture derived from its tiny seeds.

Dates
Sweet, deep brown fruit of the date palm tree, with a thick, sticky consistency resembling that of candied fruit. Sometimes pitted and chopped.

Pears
Halved, seeded and flattened fruit (below), retaining the fresh pear's distinctive profile.

Prunes
Variety of dried plum, with a rich-tasting, dark, fairly moist flesh.

Raisins
Variety of dried grapes, popular as a snack on their own. For baking, use seedless dark raisins or golden raisins (sultanas).

CURRANTS
See dried fruit.

DIJON MUSTARD
Mustard made in Dijon, France, from dark brown mustard seeds (unless otherwise marked *blanc*) and wine vinegar. Pale in color, fairly hot and sharp tasting, true Dijon mustard and non-French blends labeled "Dijon style" are widely available in supermarkets and specialty-food shops.

DILL
Herb with fine, feathery leaves and a sweet, aromatic flavor. Sold fresh or dried.

FLOUR, ALL-PURPOSE
The most common choice of flour for making muffins and quick breads, this bleached and blended (hard and soft wheats) product is available in all supermarkets. Also known as plain flour.

FLOUR, BUCKWHEAT
Flour ground from the seeds of an herbaceous plant originating in Asia; popular in the cuisines of Russia and Eastern Europe. Its strong, earthy, slightly sour flavor is usually modulated in commercial products by the addition of a little wheat flour.

FLOUR, CAKE
Very fine-textured bleached flour for use in cakes and other baked goods. Also called soft-wheat flour. All-purpose (plain) flour is not an acceptable substitute.

FLOUR, OAT
Fine flour ground from dried oats with a characteristic nutlike flavor. Used in combination with wheat flour.

FLOUR, RYE
Fine flour ground from grains of rye grass, a close relative of wheat, with a slightly sweet-sour flavor.

FLOUR, WHOLE-WHEAT
Brown-colored flour milled from whole, unbleached wheat berries. Also known as wholemeal flour.

GINGER
The rhizome of the tropical ginger plant, which yields a sweet, strong-flavored spice. Whole ginger rhizomes, commonly but mistakenly called roots, may be purchased fresh in a supermarket or vegetable market. Ginger pieces are available crystallized or candied in specialty-food shops or supermarket baking sections, or preserved in syrup in specialty shops or Asian food sections. Ground, dried ginger is easily found in jars or tins in the supermarket spice section.

GRITS
Also known as hominy grits, a fine-, medium- or coarse-ground meal derived from hominy, hulled and dried corn kernels that are a specialty of the American South.

HAZELNUTS
See nuts.

HONEY
Provides a distinctive mellow sweetness in muffin and quick bread recipes. When substituting honey for sugar in a recipe, reduce other liquids by ¼ cup (2 fl oz/60 ml) for every 1 cup (12 oz/375 g) of honey used, to compensate for the honey's higher moisture content, and reduce baking temperature by 25°F (15°C) to prevent burning.

HUBBARD SQUASH
See winter squash.

KASHA
Oven-toasted, hulled grains of buckwheat—either whole or coarse, medium or finely ground—enjoyed for their full, nutlike, slightly sour flavor.

MAPLE SYRUP
Syrup made from boiling the sap of the maple tree, with an inimitably rich savor and intense sweetness. Buy maple syrup that is labeled "pure," rather than a blend.

NUTMEG
Popular baking spice that is the hard pit of the fruit of the nutmeg tree. May be bought already ground or, for fresher flavor, whole.

Whole nutmegs may be kept inside special nutmeg graters, which include hinged flaps that conceal a storage compartment.

Freshly grate nutmeg as needed, steadying one end of grater on work surface. Return unused portion of whole nutmeg to compartment.

MOLASSES
Thick, robust-tasting, syrupy sugarcane by-product of sugar refining. Light molasses results from the first boiling of the syrup; dark molasses from the second boiling.

NINE-GRAIN CEREAL
Coarse-textured, earthy-tasting uncooked breakfast cereal, usually containing cracked rye, barley, rice, corn, oats, millet, flax, soy and triticale. If unavailable, substitute any uncooked multigrain cereal.

OAT BRAN
See bran.

OATMEAL
Coarse-, medium- or fine-textured cereal ground from hulled oats, prized for its nutlike taste and texture when cooked as a breakfast porridge or added to baked goods. Use regular rolled oats for baking—not quick-cooking or instant—unless otherwise specified.

OLIVES, GREEK
Salty cured black olives, usually packed dry or in oil. Available in ethnic delicatessens, specialty-food shops and well-stocked supermarkets. Substitute good-quality Italian black olives.

OREGANO
Aromatic and pungent Mediterranean herb—also known as wild marjoram—used fresh or dried as a seasoning for all kinds of savory dishes. Especially popular with tomatoes and other vegetables.

NUTS
Nuts such as almonds, hazelnuts (also known as filberts), peanuts, pecans, pistachios and walnuts add a wealth of flavor and texture to muffins and quick breads.

To Toast Nuts
Preheat an oven to 325°F (165°C). Spread the nuts—here, walnuts—in a single layer on a baking sheet and toast in the oven until they just begin to change color, 5–10 minutes. Remove from the oven and let cool to room temperature.

To Chop Nuts
Spread the nuts in a single layer on a nonslip cutting surface. Using a chef's knife, carefully chop the nuts with a gentle rocking motion of the blade.

Alternatively, put a handful or two of nuts in a food processor fitted with the metal blade and use a few rapid off-on pulses to chop the nuts to desired consistency; repeat with the remaining nuts in batches.

PARMESAN
Hard, thick-crusted Italian cow's milk cheese with a sharp, salty, full flavor resulting from at least two years of aging. Buy in block form, to grate fresh as needed, rather than already grated. The finest Italian variety is designated parmigiano-reggiano.

PECANS
See nuts.

PISTACHIOS
See nuts.

POPPYSEEDS
Small, spherical, blue-black seeds of a form of poppy; traditionally used in central and Eastern European cooking to add rich, nutlike flavor to baked goods.

POTATO STARCH
Also known as potato flour, a fine-textured flour ground from

potatoes that have been cooked and dried. Available in health-food stores and Eastern European shops.

PUMPKIN
See winter squash.

ROSEMARY
Mediterranean herb, used either fresh or dried, with a strong aromatic flavor. Especially complements poultry or lamb.

SAGE
Pungent herb, used fresh or dried, that goes particularly well with pork, ham or poultry.

SHORTENING, VEGETABLE
Solid vegetable fat sometimes used in place of or in combination with butter in batters. The fat is said to "shorten" the flour, that is, to make it flaky and tender.

SUGAR, BROWN
A rich-tasting, fine-textured granulated sugar combined with molasses in varying quantities to yield light or dark varieties. Widely available in supermarket baking sections.

SUGAR, CONFECTIONERS'
Finely powdered granulated sugar, combined with a little cornstarch to keep it dry and free flowing. Also called icing sugar.

SWISS CHEESE
Firm whole-milk cheese, pale creamy yellow in color, with distinctive holes that grow larger and more numerous with ripening. Popular, on its own or in recipes, for its mild, slightly sweet, nutlike flavor.

THYME
Fragrant, clean-tasting, small-leaved herb used fresh or dried as a seasoning for poultry, light meats, seafood or vegetables.

TOMATOES, SUN-DRIED
When sliced crosswise or halved, then dried in the sun, tomatoes develop an intense, sweet-tart flavor and a pleasantly chewy texture that enhance savory recipes. Available either packed in oil or dry, in specialty-food shops and well-stocked supermarkets.

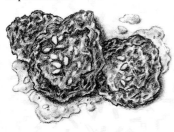

VANILLA EXTRACT
Flavoring derived by dissolving the essential oil of the vanilla bean in an alcohol base. Use only products labeled "pure" or "natural" vanilla extract (essence). Sold in specialty-food shops and supermarkets.

WALNUTS
See nuts.

WINTER SQUASH
The pale yellow to deep orange flesh of hard, tough-skinned winter squashes such as acorn, butternut, Hubbard or pumpkin makes a colorful, flavorful addition to muffins and quick breads. Before use in recipes, the squash must be cooked and mashed.

Using a heavy, sharp kitchen knife, cut the squash—here, an acorn squash—in half. If its skin is very hard, use a kitchen mallet to tap the knife carefully once it is securely wedged in the squash.

Using a sharp-edged teaspoon or tablespoon, scrape out all seeds and fibers from each squash half.

Place the squash halves, cut sides down, in a shallow baking dish and add water to reach ½–1 inch (12 mm–2.5 cm) up the sides of the squash.

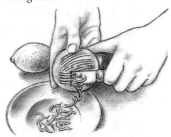

Bake in a 350°F (180°C) oven until tender, 45 minutes–1 hour, adding more boiling water if necessary to maintain original water level.

Let squash stand at room temperature until cool enough to handle. Drain well, then scoop soft flesh from each shell half into a bowl. Mash with a fork or a potato masher until smooth.

WHEAT BRAN
See bran.

WHEAT GERM
The embryo, or growing portion, of the whole wheat kernel, rich in oil and vitamin E, removed during the milling of white **flour** but left intact in whole-wheat (wholemeal) varieties. Also sold separately, often lightly toasted, small flakes of wheat germ add a wholesome, nutlike taste and slightly crunchy texture to baked goods.

ZEST
Thin, brightly colored, outermost layer of a citrus fruit's peel, containing most of its aromatic essential oils—a lively source of flavor in baking. Zest may be removed using one of two easy methods:

1. Use a simple tool known as a zester, drawing its sharp-edged holes across the fruit's skin to remove the zest in thin strips. Alternatively, use a fine hand-held grater.

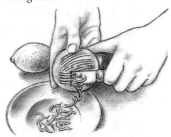

2. Holding the edge of a paring knife or vegetable peeler away from you and almost parallel to the fruit's skin, carefully cut off the zest in thin strips, taking care not to remove any white pith with it. Then thinly slice or chop on a cutting board.

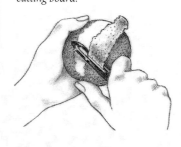

Index

ACKNOWLEDGMENTS

The publishers would like to thank the following people and organizations for
their generous assistance and support in producing this book:
Margaret D. Fallon, Jonathan C. Slater, Amy Morton, Ken DellaPenta, Sharon-Ann C. Lott,
Stephen W. Griswold, the buyers for Gardener's Eden, and the buyers and store
managers for Pottery Barn and Williams-Sonoma stores.

The following kindly lent props for the photography: Forrest Jones, Galisteo,
Stephanie Greenleigh, Philippe Henry de Tessan, Sue Fisher King, Karen Nicks,
Lorraine & Judson Puckett, Gianfranco Savio, Sue White and Chuck Williams.